Antjie Krog

Body Bereft

UMUZI

With grateful acknowledgement to the
University of the Western Cape

Published by Umuzi,
an imprint of Penguin Random House South Africa (Pty) Ltd
Company Reg No 1953/000441/07
The Estuaries No 4, Oxbow Crescent, Century Avenue, Century City, 7441, South Africa
PO Box 1144, Cape Town, 8000, South Africa
umuzi@penguinrandomhouse.co.za

Andries Wessels translated 'manifesto of a grandma' and 'Four seasonal
observations of Table Mountain'
and Gus Ferguson 'it might have been a jellytot'.

First edition 2006
Reprinted 2017, 2018, 2019
ISBN 10: 1-4152-0012-2
ISBN 13: 978-1-4152-0012-4

Cover design by Georgia Demertzis
Cover photograph by David Goldblatt
Author photograph by Pieter Hugo
Design and layout by Nazli Jacobs
Set in Walbaum

Printed and bound by Novus Print, a Novus Holdings comapny

FSC www.fsc.org MIX Paper from responsible sources FSC® C022948

Contents

PART ONE

marital song 1

since
birth our faces have been turned towards each other
as one calls the names of friends in the dark
so we called until someone answered

laudable is the word which awakens weathered
laudable is the word which, unbeknownst, falls to a whisper
laudable is the sound in which we're together as 'you' and 'I'
praiseworthy is the word 'we'

we are learning how to decline love into dialects of light
we are learning to translate empathy into saving parts of speech
'unconditional' we inscribe as preposition

it has been written that all of us will change like words
in the future tense   as well as in the past tense
in plural   as well as in loneliness
we are into the perfect tense

and are learning how blood turns into blindness
when the heart shines into it – how the perplexed glow
of happiness pulses past participles

because the earth celebrates love. belovéds and worn-out lovers
are celebrated like wine so that none of us would forget
how the dew of the world sings and sings the body's shadow

assembled here, let us praise the transient arms
let us praise the mortal fractures
let us honour this hail of whole-heartedness

the tables where we sit down are prepared with abundance
we write with our fingers the letters of the names
one by one we will write every one – to be anointed

since

since we started walking
this road the irises have
finished blooming the still
abandoned eyeballs of the
light blue ones, the plush
folded bats of the purple

row. since we started this
road the grass has been gasping
away seed, the buttercups have
dropped their leaves like nail
clippings, the camellia's
bathrobe among the cedars

has withered from the
branches since we started
the road. the tough pony-
tails of the wisteria
have fallen into disrepute
the banksia-waterfall

has finished her fatal
plunge since we started
walking this road. the
swallows have come back we
can smell the jasmine from
its jugular, the snow has

melted from the mountains.
since we started a man
tumbled backwards into
the air   what we breathe
is the air of all this
world the sky overwhelmed

as a witness of grief. at
dusk we become dark
of tongue as we translate
disintegration our
ankles reek mortal but
god how strong our thighs have

become since we walked this
road how fierce how savage
our filigree as the
heart bangs its terror

it is true

it is true that this landscape will
continue to exist without me the trees
that make me adore the earth the plains
that sweep into seams of light-lipped
water that mirrors the nearest
seams of touch the moon living
off a stipend of new born stars
it is true that it will continue to exist

it is true that I saw three women
naked on the beach at Marseilles their
bodies like three bags of wrinkles their hair
like tissues in the wind. with short steps they
padded into the water their breasts wrinkle-less
forming a halo of flesh of steaming risen
breasts blushing into their nipples it is
true that I couldn't keep my eyes off them

it is true that I saw in a shop window three
kinds of nappies for the aged, bedpans,
fungicide, bedsore ointments and something
that looked like a potato peeler it is true that
as of late I stare intensely at old people how
they put their feet down or wear their hair that I
lay my eyes desperately on young skin and fluent
bodies it is true that I'm on the brink of an abyss

seven menopausal sonnets

it rumbles softly

it rumbles softly. the earth lifts her skull.
a thunderstorm curls from the inner wing
of clouds all along the silent palate of
mountains. a bulbul slips into the most

intimate place of the maple tree – there
where the trunk keeps its most quiet
quietness. motionless the tree waits as
lightning streams in from levels of blue

as the veld yields her skin towards
skies fragrant with covenant. roses bleed
in her hair. when the last coolness damps from

her armpits, she unfastens her long heart. never
had she been so meager, so lonely, or had
yearned for rain that simply didn't, never came

like death in my arms

you come and sit this morning like death in my arms
I am so tired I can hardly breathe. you say
what has been promised by whom?
what is written in the weathering of our bodies?
our life together walks its own destructive road
I am independent and totally unreliable you say
I am tired of being questioned, of being watched, tested
I say you are fed up being lied to with frantic explanations

and I? I want nothing   I do not want to be anything
to anybody   I do not want to belong anywhere   I want
to fall free – suddenly and colourless like a stone

one thing I'm learning
the more I destroy you the more
I myself am run into the ground

bronze bull of Lavigny

the upright stance is wearing him down
the forever-young torso is getting to him
his over-indulged chest is slipping in between
his legs as he drags the blonde fields uphill in

a remembered act of bliss – his hide skinned
by seasons of poets feeling him up for metaphors
his balls rust forth, his thighs shuffle
protectively around the sweet decomposing

chamber of lust. what is he to do now – this
sad solitary bull? his tail sprained. one horn
gone. his body has become one dumb
eroding dump of fear among the trees. he

knows the great collapse is here and pushes his dry
derelict snout up among the mauve pertblue plums

short visit

the child is leaving. I'm left standing.
well-known eyes meet before the sunglasses.
hands grapple while the safety belt.
the street desolate. I wave, wave. as

all light pales. as everything aspires
bleaker. as the heart refuses.
everything that should have been said.
after every visit I devise.

next time to explain the scorching.
I undertake ways.
I utter what binds us. you want to

hear so little. the unsaid bloodshot desperate
fistblow. whether it had hit the snout.
full out. jesus! I am bleeding, child

sonnet of the hot flushes

something staples your marrow somewhere
you feel a newly floated fire spreading angst from
a kernel and how your veins run with fire how
your flesh flames your heart keeps her fireproof
balance your bones bake besides themselves your
face singes your cheeks simmer in dismay and
time and again you break out in sizzling encasings
of sweat you smell your skin sparking off a blaze.

But one day you shift in your chair – and
feel this enormous crucible destroying your
last juiciness. God knows, this is enough:
burning like a warrior you rise – a figurehead of
fire – you grab death like a runt and plough its nose
right through your fleeced and drybaked cunt

hormone sonnet

to hrt
or not to hrt
is a question
only for women

it implies: do you want to look younger,
get cancer and Alzheimer's
or do you want to look old
and live too long?

if I ask my mother about menopause
she looks at me as if I've said the word 'internet'
'didn't you ever get hot flushes?'

'my girl, when I sweated I assumed
it was from work and then I went
swimming or sommer took a shower'

on my behalf

i no longer need to approach anybody on someone's behalf
i no longer need to be accountable for others
or to ask forgiveness on behalf of those who know no guilt

i no longer need to put anybody's marginalised
perspective on the table or imagine
myself into the skin of another

because the first forays of death have arrived
and the body slips like sand through
the fingers. apathy neutralises the senses

as survival deploys its brutal forces. one gets cut
off from others and becomes more and more
familiar with the complete inward-turning of death –

drawer after drawer you are being emptied out
until only your empty inside moves your emptiness about

God, Death, Love

God, Death, Love, Loneliness, Man
are Important Themes in Literature
menstruation, childbirth, menopause, puberty
marriage are not

meanwhile terror lies exactly in how
one lives with the disintegrating body
in how one accepts that the body no longer
wants to intensify with exhilarating detonations

in how one loves the more-and-more-slaked-ones
in how one resigns to vaginal atrophy and incontinence
or that the blade cleaving through one's heart
is probably a heart attack

to jump from the ageing body to Death
has suddenly become a cop-out act

leave me a lonely began

> 'the voice of the menopausal woman is feared
> and denied. She has been made invisible or
> encouraged to remain forever young . . .' – *Tamara Slayton*

he sits across, reading his newspaper
his coffee waits timorously next
to his precisely clipped nails. his
hairy ear busting with gunpowder. his

shaven cheeks brittle. suddenly he looks
up and shouts to the back: 'coffee shop's
empty, we can close!' and she realises: he
does not see her. she sits as nothing. that where she

is is simply air or glass or emptiness
he did not *not* see her, or perchance look
past – he looked right *through* her. she's
vanished without tamper or trauma;

to the waiter she's merely table-leg or chair
how did it come to this where nothing
exists any longer that acknowledges her
as a woman? nothing that recognises

that she carries the cool shape of a human
who loves the earth and this late coffee
on the square where soft seeds waft
the midday air? her silent invisibility

bends her eyes to her hand playing
with crumbs on the blue check table
cloth. and it is so: every finger joint
is thickened and stiffening into a

new direction. next to the swollen vein
in an unguarded moment, a brown
stain was deftly stapled. it is as if great
and dull boulders fill her from the

inside and she withholds her from
herself as if from a grater. *this* she knows:
nobody will ever again breathlessly
peel desire from her shoulders.

when tight is loose

it must have happened gradually, but
she feels overcome – suddenly her body
is simply loose, as if nothing wants
to be firmly tied and trim. for example
her teeth, hair, everything down to her
pelvic floor is now loose, even her

eyes bubble – the left one with its own
eccentric jumpiness. here is the upper lip
plying the accordion and yesterday when
she pointed at something, her upper arm
flapped its own new suede purse –
her thumbs are crumbling away and refuse

to open bottles, taps or masturbate.
her stomach lies like a dish in her lap.
there are blue medallions on her thighs
and if she *has* to look down, she sees
her knees shrinking like forgotten
prunes in a bowl. her skin is loose from

her flesh like a shuddered boiled-milk
skin. what should be tight, is loose
and what should be loose is very
tight, because if she looks left all
her shoulders simply have to turn as well;
it is last year she saw her haunches last

in the *Hormone Book* by Susan Mare
she reads about the wane
of oestrogen: the waist thickens and
the vagina wall thins and the colon crashes
through its own arse. how dare her toe-
nails grow so riotous then, thicken so

yellowish while she is loosening at the
seams and simply falling away? since
when has her blood impulse changed
from 'fuck off ' to 'careful now'?
since when have her transgressions
fallen back to half a zol? since

when has her memory gone more than
it comes? since when has she been aware that
the brain is looking for bridges across
the dying of nerve ends at the outer
edges of the skin? since when have the tiny
sprouts in the ear been calcifying and

the retina lost its ability to delight
in bright colours? when did the brain
let go of the slaked tongue? why does
the nose yearning for youth have
to muffle forth with an expired prostate?
mornings her piss smells like wet cement

marital song 2

your everyday daily hand in mine
the silence of your thumb
and a palm that is always itself

your hand secretes a mildness
which I fail to name adequately
if you hold me I breathe

our love lords the place
as you weigh in with me until
words convert guile into a glow

of startling light; you can lift me on stilts
and so sterling, dearest, things seldom appear to me.
from the edges you pull me back

and convince me to here-ness
to righteousness
for nobody's name's sake

nobody humans language more than you
nobody ignites like you
across borders of leaving and loss

seamless you fathom, fearless you point
the rot. out of all you have chosen me
but in the meantime you have turned grey

and awkwardly vulnerable in your sheath
for myself you took me in and forged me legitimate
from deep within my lungs I care for you

your integrity fills the length of our love
my eyes open up all around you
I bequeath my mouth to you

you have searched me and known me
you know my downsitting and mine uprising
you understand my heart afar off

but your hand now, this afternoon
thoughtfully in mine, reveals
that we are one flesh and that

you will die, like me
and like me,
you will do it alone

and not even death, beloved,
can sunder us
in this

morning tea

while she makes tea something strangely
familiar flows down her inner thigh. like ink.
after many years she bleeds again.

she stands overcome – as if a whole orchard
blossoms up in her throat, as if an old-fashioned
happiness leaks into her body. she feels she's

opening shutters towards apples, towards
shades that haze with birds and cicadas
and sweltering distances – as if a

child's laughter overflows in a bath
turning her cheeks vulnerable – intimately
blushed through with daily closeness

as if her abdomen swells young and
strong again around the most beautiful that
she was; her neck gives in to so much light

she carries the tea out onto the stoep
the sky slakes soft for this time of the
morning; the city glistens like a brimming dam

he comes to sit next to her. peacefully he
stirs his tea. in this way they sit
so far left behind in loss and for their age

so carefully rare in closeness

how do you say this

I truly don't know how to say this
your seasoned neatly clipped beard is perhaps
too here, too close for language, too grey with grit

I really don't know how to write your ageing body
without using words like 'loss' or 'fatal'. I don't know.
I don't know why the word 'wrinkle' sounds so banal
I simply do not know how ageing should sound in language

in the meantime the irises of your infamous blue eyes
have over the years buckled under green
more stuttering now but two enduring sincere

shadows that have loved me a whole life long
my forefinger traces your eyebrows
from where grey hair crackles like lightning.
face that I love; face of erosion

if I pull you towards me your hair is thin and light
your scalp surprises me with its own texture
the grooves cutting down from your ears

the mouth that could scathe so brilliantly still
moves fragrantly against my temples but mild now
– as bread. your hands allow my breasts to sink into
your palms like glasses of dark wine. I think I'm

trying to say that I find the thickening of your
abdomen attractive, that an erection against a
slight curve leaves one wet in the mouth. god,

I think I'm trying to say that I can surrender to
your thighs for the very first time because of
their soaking whiteness, that I prefer the soft
looseness of your buttocks to the young hard

aggressive passion of our youth. you no longer
use sex for yourself but for me. you no longer
want to breed children from me but calmly reveal

yourself. into the luxury of experience I
stretch myself out. it is as if you are deeper, as if I'm
quieter, as if we come to be much more complete.
at times it seems easier to rage

against the dying of the light
than to eke out
the vocabulary of old age

manifesta of a grandma

Casually you ask, 'So how does it feel to be
a grandma?' and I thought to myself, oh god,
my child, what would you have me say?
'. . . very old thank you'? or 'I don't
get cock past my lips anymore'? I mean, what

does one say? More important perhaps is why
a question like this makes me so the moer in?
Do I suffer from excessive vanity or am I ashamed
of my early breeding ability . . .? But really,
deep down, I know: it roots in the word 'grandma'.

'Grandma' has such a poo sound, sounds so blubbery
so almost tubbery, it mumbles so cuntless, so toothless
inaudibly that it rips your nose wide open for
grandma-bashing and suddenly you smell the entire
written media unaware of wild yam and hrt.

Children's books are full of modern moms with clogs
buying pizzas and dads bathing babies, but in the
background somewhere inevitably lurks misshapen
a grandma anachronistically in Dr Scholl's shoes
joyously knitting – spectacled and bunned. A bun

for fuck's sake! My own children don't even know anyone
with a bun, not to mention my culturally mixed-up
grandchildren! Sometimes a grandpa fumbles along with stick,
coat and grey felt hat, (grey what?) – a surprised expression on his face
suggesting that throughout life he has peered only through bifocals.

A headline announces: 'High jump record for grandma'.
What does it really suggest? For a grandma
she jumps rather high? How high is a grandma
entitled to jump? Or should she indeed jump
but not over a bar in public?

'Grandma of three sues premier for sexual harassment'.
What is the message here? That a grandma should actually
be grateful that someone still wants to fondle her
or that the premier must really be desperate
to molest a grandma to get his rocks off?

Note that the premier himself is presented with neither
kith nor cunt. The head Scorpion states that he will not
jail Winnie Mandela, because grandmas don't belong in
jails. Grandpas can go to jail, but no grandmas. No
dammit! I claim my right to the dignity of inmate.

At Pick 'n Pay I stop behind a kombi from the Sunset Home.
Gingerly they emerge – no spectacles or buns in sight.
Short-clipped hair, running shoes for shopping.
Nimbly a gent hops from the passenger seat – in one hand
his aluminium strut, with the other he smoothes his ponytail.

Then it strikes me: the primal source of my aversion
to the word 'grandma' comes from the
well-known children's rhyme 'Grandpa and Grandma'*
on that bloody stoep with their errant sphincters.

Grandma asks Grandpa, 'What was that roar?' Grandpa
sighs euphemistically, 'My tummy's sore.'
Then Grandma asks (of all fucking things she asks):
'A pear for the pain?!' whereupon Grandpa draws
a highly scientific conclusion:

'Then I'll fart again.' For ever and ever in three
rhyming couplets metred in the falling
rhythm of dactyls this senile hogwash of stoepsitters
is conveyed from generation to generation
as the very essence of grandpa- and grandmahood

'So what did you ask?
You asked about being a grandma? Lovely, my dear,
absolutely lovely – as you can see:
Grandpa and I here on the stoep
– we take it lying down.'

Translated by Andries Wessels

* This refers to an obscene Afrikaans children's rhyme, cherished by generations of small children as their first encounter with subversive text:

Oupa en Ouma sit op die stoep,	Grandpa and Grandma sit on the stoep
Oupa gee 'n harde poep.	Grandpa farts with an enormous whoop.
Ouma vra: 'Wat makeer?'	Grandma asks, 'What was that roar?'
Oupa sê: 'My maag is seer.'	Grandpa says, 'My tummy's sore.'
Ouma sê: 'Eet 'n peer.'	Grandma asks, 'A pear for the pain?'
Oupa sê: 'Dan poep ek weer.'	Grandpa says, 'Then I'll fart again.'

writing ode

> 'Writing is a fraught activity for everyone, of course, male or female, but women writers seem to have to take stronger measures, make more peculiar psychic arrangements, than men' – Janet Malcolm: *The Silent Woman*

to be able to write one has to enter the self
    by going beyond the limits imposed by the self

one has to leave the daylight
the drag of fabricated voices
    and go underground

one travels like a thought

it is quiet there
and completely cut-off
safe   private
one touches down the damp inside
one gropes through the groundless dark
    to find one's voice
to hear the sound of a poem
the line that softly sputters from somewhere

and the writing, the writing down, takes place
    in wrestling the self down

(the man that one loves
waits at ground level
Sundays when late afternoon light slips into stone
he walks against the mountain slopes
the spaces that are not
are not, he says)

this problematises the writing down
and one enters a duel with the self

    *

the earth groans in the colour of rust
the sun spatters brittle blue fires
where then is the word initially safe?
where can it be given an impartial birth
before it is tested, tuned and packed for ground level?

(the vineyard against the slopes
takes a consummate green oath
that nothing will go to pieces
under this tightly-stretched wind-blown sky
on moonlit nights you can hear the hoofs
sparking stars from the stones
but what do these lines say?
how much colour is sheafed into them?)

*

I awake somewhere else with a mouth full of lovely words
he, my love
is my heart's rush and refuge
I simply want a life with him

I do washing in a bath
I am on ground level
I walk out on this morning brisk of pelvis
    and with steadfast calves
    into the small backyard thrilled by sun
suddenly
    to be dazed by the fragrance of figtree
    soap and stone
    the sandpaper leaves and devastating copper

like you I belong to the earth
and the scars thereof

*

love flatters in diverse vestiges
but there is space for everybody underground
    as middle-aged shadows of each other
until he gets up from the round green chair and says:
I've had enough
and takes down his suitcase
and it becomes dark all around
and one claws up towards light don't
don't let go of us like this
from fall to fall it doesn't matter
but
here it does it does
ever

one writes: the light licks your face clean
silver in its tips
you give yourself away with your eyes

one writes: this is a morning to die
against his blameless neck under the bluegums
reeling towards his heretical mouth

one writes: you eat as if you feast
I'm frightened by my hunger for your planed ankles
the earth is warm with little frogs

one has everything to lose
one gives up nothing
one balances among wounds, scabs and scar tissue

*

the text shudders into its unfettered form underground
one cuts it neatly loose and takes it up
where it plunges one into autumn abruptly
clear
unscathed
leaves sift like coals from the burning trees

*

you were the inconvenient
    and irrefutably too late love of my life

I *dare* not have underground
I *can not* live upper ground
from everywhere channels run deep
I search on the wind for a voice to you
my life lies like stone

words do not manage to leave you
words do not manage to keep you
cold bites up from the grass
behind my scarf I say your name your name
and the wind cuts snow

never are you out of my thoughts
you give everything skin
    as my life slips away into yours

it had never been difficult
your body is of colour
and nowhere do you keep back from me
I know you more intimately than a snare or silk or twine

*

how can I unlearn you
if only I could hold on tighter

*

at times one grows tired of naming
of fighting the angry self down
as underground grief becomes grave

*

grab me, hold my heart
I come not loose from you
I wish you here, your hand turned slightly
for ever against the winter fibre of my cheek
I enter this ice age – alone
with the thin blue line of mountains in the distance

it's over, you are saying
underground from where I am returning
after having lived a futile landscape
not here
here not ever

*

I no longer function on ground level
I am past all caring
everything breaks loose
what have I lost here?
what do I want here
in this place
where I'm always absent?

it's a morning made for death
I have given up my heart
I live only in my nails

where sleeps my belovéd tonight?

*

in the meantime it has become winter
one pounds you into the skeleton of one's heart
supported and suddenly prepared
    one bundles you voetstoots underground
your eyes bleach before memory snaps tight

one's heart blows out her last breath
it's the time of endings
never has one loved him so much
as the moment one left him

*

his eyes weather into frames of sadness
his ponytail laced with tuberose slips through my palm
I miss him
    however many are the days
and the word is grieve

where sleeps my belovéd, who calms his rue?
where sleeps my belovéd, where sleeps he true?

I walk down foreign streets
my hands deep in my pockets
my body will never forgive me for this

what is left?

god, what does he do on this morning
is he standing forlorn in our white kitchen
hoarse next to the last roses?

*

I peel your face
I bite your tongue like a banana from your mouth
burning your language crashes into me

I turn away scorched
the trees are so livid in foreign countries
as your eyes drift towards me in exorbitant light

with you, loveliness and slumber
    are more fundamental than betrayal
the earth rears softly at our feet
in order to belong I went to fetch you
in this geometrical foot of groundlevel space
I touch nothing any more as if it is mine

I want to know where the belovéd sleeps tonight?

here or there
groundlevel or lower?
I want to go back to the places where I made us
something in me grew up to find you
and in that moment anguish turned into sound
that endures from then
until now
do not go away
ever from me

*

(you could have
decided not to desire
to avert
to learn to forget
another skin
you could have)

but when the earth talks to herself
everything desires long feathered wings

*

after months the underground tunnel
    digs into light
blindly I douse the sun with soft paws
and hear your glad near-sighted laugh: you're here
you're here
ruined we hold on to each other
the earth I can not bear without you

you sleep, yes
you have come to sleep in me
and your sleep holds everything
you will never sink out of me again
through my word you have stepped into my breath
with your bony mouth

past our ageing bodies and lost scars
we hold each other
we sink to the ground
we see the face of our dying:

*

and now one can say it
(in one's fought-for language):
it is here that one's belovéd sleep tonight!
and one can call all whom one loves
and say:
see
the trees stand drenched with mortality
    everything weeps with transience

*

I fling our eyes like burning coals into the cold
airily I brush the knuckle of your middlefinger
before us and after us
listen
how the doves drown their sound in the heat
let us breathe carefully past our bruises
death slobbers at our heels

we know that everything will die
all writing and all things written
but this earth
this drizzled breathtaking blue taffeta of earth
not

we touch with newer tenderness

we want to last to watch the earth
and hone language to hold the moment

in this graced word
we belong with each other

touch me
tonight
my decomposing cheek with your fingertip tendril

songs for the most recently arrived

1.
subdued light bleeds through the half-open door
when you report in glass   breathlight and
heartbreakwhole you surprise us in the night
your first cry plummets my body and my
heart hits the earth. your shoulders stretch and
strain   such a distance you've had to come
to make boer and jew calibrate. how unharmed
you are, how you smell of fresh boracic lint.
we bind you in our arms as our tiniest sheaf
of light and peppermint. we host you
in honey, love, from fynbos we dream a tent

but as I hold you my breastbone
rears with pain   then crashes forward
in sparks of flame and firmament

2.

the abundance of her tiny skull we do not
grasp. under her hair, one by one
small leaves fold to bone so that her
little face like a lamp overflows with

light and we can see the rose syllables
of her hands or the rustle of a smile
as it glides up into her newborn eyes
to prevail upon them to stay in this

valley of breath. her feet ladling a glow
as we lay her down in milk and fold
her tight. from so many selves

she's had to salvage her selfest self
before she could arrive as our
tiniest bullet of belovéd light

3.

in the great eternal pulse
of time, in the solemn tread
of history it is irrelevant
that last night your tiny heel

was in my palm – stone-cool
rinse-calm. the instep as form
tapped into my heart while I assist you
in escaping your mother's call

from my outstretched hand your heel tore
a wing of lace – I licked the blood from my
wrist while light-footed and slender-limbed
you bounced off into space

aliya

1.
you leave tomorrow for
Isra-el
with your mother
for good

when we see each other
in a
year's time you will speak only
Hebrew.

in my searing memory where
you slip
lank and lovely with
stem-light

ankles and ribbons in-
to lakes
of sheen we will not
find one word

awake. speechless we
will stare
at each other. in
your deep

tradition people tear
their clothes.
I ache from the
spleen

2.
I wanted to create an ark in my arms
in which you could be whole
the whole time – where faultlines
could dissolve into gentleness

and olive branch; where your eyes
could be smoothed back into inkblack
your legs be moved to the windward
of the word carefree, where your fits

of crying and anger could be calmed.
I wanted to snatch you from the
battlefield of your parents to have
and to hold. your swerve I wanted to be

and your sword. you left with the victor.
among all, *my* love did you the least harm

ode for another life

I want another life
I want to walk in other streets
I want to take a lift in another city
and step out on a new floor
I want to be in another supermarket
I want to take different food from different shelves
I want other teeth
I want to wear dresses and light-yellow sandals
I want to travel along other roads
with other mountains in my windows
I want another life

I want another space
that I don't have to share with you
so that I can be in a place
where I can again long for you
where I need not confuse longing with familiarity
I want to miss your mouth
I want to imagine your eyes
you must be in my head more than in my bed
in loved languages I want to call you forth
until I come right to you
I want another space

I want another chance
to prove to my children my
love for them (and as I write this
their faces appear as if on a monitor
screen): belovéd child
I want you to know
that your mother is moved
by your vulnerable courage
that I reel at how deep you invest in love
how delicately you deploy your uniqueness
your hands and feet
the shyness of the back of your
head and your beautiful eyes –
all of it your mother can recite by heart in the night

I want to plead for a new space
in which I can say that I love every one of you
the most (and if you need me to say
that I love *you* the most –
then I am saying it here:
among all I love you the most my child, *just* like the others)
in which I can say that what you are
keeps on astounding me
that how you are renders me proud
that in my thoughts again and again
I embrace you and hold you

allow me a space
in which my presumptuous anguish
my sharp underestimations can disappear
in which you can know
that nobody could ever love you
more liberatingly
more impedingly than I
please give me another chance

l'envoi
I want another life
in which I can touch unhampered
and love imperishably
I am tired of the deficit of my hands
my pauperising brain and tongue I no longer want
I am tired of shifting:
from how to stay young   to how to stay alive
from how to stay alive   to how to love
from how to love   to how to love to the good

I am tired of this lifelong wanting
the needing of another life

depression

1.
it's as if you are disappearing more
and more within your eyes
as if your forehead
grows darker your cheeks
more motionless your mouth
further than anything
has ever been from me your
body so transparent that my
hand goes right through you
if I try to prevent you from
disappearing you move among us
but have broken all contact from your
hands I can see at times how fiercely
you hold on the nails in your fingers
become erased it is as if I run down
a riverbank throwing life-buoys and
ropes and branches I am beside
myself I yell that you should hang
on hang in there I will salvage
you I will give myself in your
place I will rip God Almighty
Himself from heaven I'll give
anything to bring you back
safely into your eyes

2.

it's terrible seeing you like this.
how will I ever find you.
seeing you so terrible.
how do I get you back. if only I had.
if I'd rather. why didn't I.
it's terrifying. see, here I stand.
I tear. I try to tear.
how to cut my love for you.
how to cut it loose.
cut the inadequacy – gut and all.
it's terrible. how do I find you.
how do I feed into you.
how to come to you.
you are rinsed through, child.
you are lighter loveliness.
so much so that your ribs.
you have to glow of it.
that you feel mercy
in your upper-arms.
oh my God, please
be kind to yourself
you are so young. so beautiful.
you strain so lost against an earth
that God knows
has simply loved you
your whole life long
how do I get to you. it's terrible to.
it's terrible to see you.
seeing you like this.

softsift of the hourglass

1.
half of her is somebody else
as if   somebody else
is standing next to her *in* her like
the bridge of a nose   her brain
tolls and tolls and keeps on tolling
        she opens the shower   her left
        cheek soaks in the spray until warm
        inside   her right
        cheek hangs   cold and dull on
        the outside   her blood pressure
rears and rears and keeps on rearing
a chipped shoulder knob   the other
glad and gleaming   the breasts hang
wide-eyed in front of a heart which bangs blood
deafening through all the veins
        her body resounds from her lymph
        the left hand   has lost its grip
        it fumbles like a dishcloth at the soap
        the right does not know   what the left is doing
        only one hand   washes the lame
the left as egg whisk   pale stalled fountain
disintegrating mop   wilting lily
blood begins to crawl   where once it ran
        but it is the left leg
        that she misses most
        the light footed turn   the swank of swerve
        the quick sidestep in jest –
enraged she rips into everything
inside herself, but quivering in her ribs
one can see that already
she's been by the half-dead dead eclipsed

2.

It might have been a jellytot
transmogrified to fatal clot

a flake detached from an artery wall
that caused the cataclysmic squall,

the tidal tug of 'yours' and 'mine'
that made the heart a fist of pain

but doctors said a ball of slime
in evil ambush, marking time

at hint of weakness pulled the pin
(the seismic wave! the shivered skin!)

and in the bright dawn they said with a sigh:
'No more will lamb with lion lie.'

Hey nonny nonny no,
why has my body forsaken me so?

Translated by Gus Ferguson

marital song 3

1.
to think about you when you were young
when everything about you was unknown

your hair strange, your clothes new to me
your language, the smell of your tongue

but your face completely legible
and elatedly surrendering to me.

now, after thirty years our hair smells the same
our stomach linings growl around the same food

your face however no longer provides any corridors
we have become family. we are fighting

for survival together like two open mouths
we no longer know where which commences, when

what expires where within our most secret silences
at times we are still on rafts of birdsong

as if we form part of a procession of stars
as if autumn trees carry the colour of the soles of our feet

when I'm away I know the back of your
head and how impossible it is to overtake your torso

each word between us devotedly revenges itself
with the live weight of thirty years

nobody could call this a conversation
although my neck longs for your hands

and between my shoulder blades
at times lightly, your tongue

2.
misspelt and imprecisely translated
we flame forward on the breath of a country

where ageing awaits us in what we own
we do not quite know on what we shall live

together we overflow more and more towards the vulnerable
for the first time the impossible has startled us

neither may leave now
the fears multiply incessantly

we are thrown upon each other
and your body has become a sad slope

your smile in my direction so incidental
that it hardly recalls a battle order

please do not forget the hollows of my arms –
let us live our degenerate old age to the hilt

PART TWO

letter-poem lullaby for Ntombizana Atoo

1.
hush-hush
sleep-a-bye
sweet
sleep soft
sleep whole
sleep blackly tilted

childest child of mine
childling born wet   born now

outside orbits the earth
so ah and you
so softly bloused in blue

let wind take your nostrils
let earth take eyes and ears and tongue
let fire let rain take your skin

inside crackles your tongue
your fists tiny roses clenched in plum
you lie in a baylet
for the last time made holy by blood and yourself

shush now
shush now

childkin black   childkin veld
childkin nobody
to nothing ever held
childkin breast   childkin thirst

hush-hush
sleep-a-bye
sweet
sleep soft
sleep whole
sleep blackly tilted

2.

the wind is all over the sky
with my voice on its way to you
you who lies irrefutably stippled
somewhere in cloth and herb
in songlets and pain
your vertebrae curving against what's to come
hold on dear child
against it all

that you could see the earth
clinging with suns and moons and comets and meteorites
the windfiltered sky
in tufts of fire tomatoes fly out among leaves
the moon reports in milk
in the thorn trees next to the road the stars also hum their way to you
you have to see
you have to hear how the sun lures the wind over your threshold
taste how the water changes to still ivory plates in the setting sun

dear child the earth glows of heaven

3.

I will come and claim you from bones and bullets and violence and aids
from muteness from stupidity from the corrupt faces of men
I'll gather you from millions of refugees
from hunger and thirst from the damp of cries
and the stink of tolerated grief
the desperate mangle of dreams
from the back I'll recognise the brave stalk of your neck
I will catch up with you
and pull you out by the arm

because you have to see differently
for us of the abyss
we all have to balance differently
this continent drifting like a big black plundered heart on the globe
continent that is us
continent throbbing with blood in the vast ventricles of desert
and forest   savannah and stone
forlorn continent
on which so many lost figures commit lost deeds of forlorn trust
big aggressive heart on which thousands die daily without sound
decaying in heaps
into raking brooms of bones

I want it to be you my smallest
that between your ribs
you have to feel the tremor that things have to be different
that something has to become true of what we are

that what we are as Africans is something so soft so humanly skinned
so profoundly constitutionally big and light and kind as soul
so caring as to surpass all understanding

we are what we are because we are of each other

why do we keep on then being so wrong?
I lay my cheek next to yours
I want to breathe into you
to care
to care
hush
hush

4.

mould your shoulder blades into tiny wings
breast the roaming despair
lovely thing I am so close to you, your cheek lies in peach down
your necklet wobbles this side that side
next to your mother who sleeps with her head turned towards you
do you hear me?
everything is so lucid tonight
your mouth has loosened a little from the breast
do you hear me –
I who am all-that-is-white
who am lightningwhite and indissolubly always only myself?
make this continent yours
bask in your hands this morose mumbling heart
cradle it so that it splays out its clogged crooked valves
rig its full sails to the wind and navigate the earth in celebration
it has become yours
it has become mine
it is ours

dark outside
a chain rustles and I hear magazines slip off into the grass
I stop breathing and bend over you
my finger touching your fist
which slips open and holds me immediately
tightly
your mother stirs
loveliest thinniken thing I have just come to say welcome!
and that something of me will go with you
and that you needn't know of it

5.
sleep sweet
sleep soft
sleep loved and blackly tilted

sh-sh
childest childling
child of mine
child of morrow
the veld lies loose in its skin of words

little girl, with wild plaits and cheeky slender neck
it is you, one day, making poems along the dusty road
    singing forward the way

    yes! I see you

Rwanda, 2000

fossil alphabet

the found fossil does not describe
how my blue eyes look past your eyes
how your black eyes look away from my eyes
how my white forearm does not simply
    rest next to your black forearm
how my sleek hair sleeps next to your frizzy hair

the fossil does however describe in the finest vertebrae
how the coast blindingly kept on shouting
    after the continent that once was part of her
how the fynbos undisputedly sniffed for her torn-away friends
how the rusted rock along the coast longed for the drifted bloodbrother

but the fossil knows that once everything was linked
that we broached our hearts for one another
only we don't know
    why we now sit with this stoney one-ness
and so much furious aversion

prayer for the bones

. . . his back at
times . . . with the
navy jersey . . . skew

a hand movement
perhaps . . . a finger
bone was what

I had asked . . .
a sign . . .he
lives and is

okay . . . or he's
dead and in
a way okay . . .

then it can
stop . . . not-searching's
. . . endless search . . . at

the back of the
throat pain heaps
. . . perhaps

I will look
up and onto . . .
the body about

. . . I could
not yet grieve . . .
it will be

whole . . . and wholly
mine . . . no fuss . . .
I will look

only down . . . to
what I am . . .
busy with . . . you

see . . . bring them . . .
I want to . . .
see how they

look . . . they who . . .
lost human-kind
who . . . came to

harm . . . mine . . . they
can . . . bring healing . . .
I forgive before

I am asked . . .
so that they . . .
can see . . . how

a true person . . .
looks . . . so that
they can learn

human-kind
from me . . . then
we can see . . .

how a white . . .
shows that he
is . . . getting it

back . . . how
a white human
. . . looks

farewell

you drift away from me
and this strange white wrapping which fits me so well

I remember you with my arms:
because I've always been from here

I belong nowhere else
but in this boat belting in horror and blue

with my heart nailed to the mast
flapping black with you

whether you see it like this
I don't know

whether you acknowledge my right to say so
I will want to know

from you – but this journey
released me from the tyranny of one

dare light slip so soft
dare sand reel so free

dare skin say so much
in this search for identity?

skin has many colours
the heart many shapes

but when we look into the water
I get a fright from the omnipresent

white who sits like this:
stipulating truth-ness

colonialism of a special kind

1.
'I am forgiven and accepted . . .
I can continue with my life'

'I have forgiven and accepted . . .
and they continue with their lives'

'I am dumbstruck that I've been forgiven . . .
they seem not to be able even to hate effectively'

'I am dumbstruck that I have forgiven . . .
and they continue as if nothing has happened'

justice for the rich
forgiveness for the poor

people are made ashamed that they have forgiven

because at the deepest level
we respect anger
understand hate
admire revenge

2.
what happens to those who choose to live on the earth lightly
here today gone tomorrow
the only trace they leave
is the language of grass and trees

what becomes of them?

what becomes of those who choose to care for other people?
who always look for the human in rich and poor
who cannot endure that other people suffer

what becomes of them?

the earth and the fullness thereof
the world and those who live in it
belong to the mighty

what becomes of them?

Dommelfei / crone in the woods

she no longer reads books
they have nothing to say
to her. she no longer listens

to music   it makes her
restless and fills her with longing
she no longer watches television

as it witnesses a world
in which she no longer has
a say. no children

can come from her any
more and she refuses to raise
those of others

she has no interest in the inner
power mechanisms of men
powerful men revolt her

young men they bore her
old men render her sad
a red-hooded grandchild

with sturdy legs is on the
way towards her. she has sloughed
the demands of gender and behaviour

like an apron
and rides her life out
like a song.

*

she gets up when it's light
she goes to bed when it's dark
she lives within the crush of stars
and the moon a luminous
presence on the stoep

for the withering of her ovaries
she uses mixtures of primrose oil, soya-
flakes and clover. with tinctures of
black cohosh and wild yams she
loosens the streptococcus from her glands

with ginseng she smoothes knuckles
with blouslangkop and sweet sedge
she brews a special tea
to tap cancer from the breasts. she
wets her dahlias with early morning pee

a blue crane walks with her as she
picks wild geranium for unguents
forest sage for new infusions –
an eagle with a single wingtip
cuts her line of vision.

she'll knead your thighs, she'll minister your
upper arms with balms. your forsaking heart
your flaking skin, she'll comfort. she'll unfasten
your mind and preserve your tongue gently
in the lower jaw. and when she sends you

alone into the cold wind of ageing
you'll be searing from the marrow-bone.

the indigent

1.
while she closes her purse
his shadow drifts to the left of her hand
while she reverses from her parking space
he gesticulates wildly next to her
as she walks down to the café
he moves from under a piece of cardboard
while she prunes her roses, he asks for water

while she stacks the dishwasher
he stands at the gate
while she marks exam papers he rings the front doorbell
he asks old clothes, empty bottles
money for a taxi, money for a funeral
money for his children, money for his mother

while she sleeps, he scratches in trashcans
while she makes coffee
he shits on the steps between Buxton and Rosmead
while she goes for a walk
he stumbles to his feet among the sugarbush
at the traffic light it becomes eye to eye combat
to conquer or protect fields of vision

should she again buy coat hangers or wire animals from the Senegalese
or should she rather support Big Issue
or should she simply give money to the glue-sniffing boy
or is the one on the city council crutches her man
or should she rather wait until the next corner
to give to the mother with the child on her back in this pollution
or the begging dwarf at the four-way stop in Upper Orange

outside the supermarket two fight to push her trolley
three claim they have been guarding her car
in front of her house a small gang who washed her car
waits for money and food
on the terrace at Carlucci's the begging voice of the woman gets louder
somebody puts a rose on the table and asks for money
over the phone somebody collects money for the deaf
by mail World Vision collects for Mthetheleli

while she dishes soup she tries to think: icy water pushes through the shacks
in front of the heater she tries to remember: they are all scurrying for the only bed
at the Modderdam and De la Rey Street crossing
they wait in silent rows for piece jobs
in Harrington Street they stand in silent rows at the soup kitchen
in St George's Mall they lie in silent rows passed out from cold, hunger or glue

the poor are coming towards her
from the four corners of the earth
they crowd on the plains
and climb onto the mountain terraces
whatever she does they will be with her
and her inability to live a life in proportion to them
even her smallest action will be without honour

(Bertolt Brecht said that it was only those who knew hunger
who would feed the hungry
        – the rich feed only each other)

will her larynx ever become bone
enough to stand with the poor and shout:

'Destroy the ramparts the barricades the walls the malls
let us build shacks in the backyards, plant maize in the parks
sleep in the cars, eat on the stoeps, appropriate and populate flats and hotels
yes, let us stir pap in the cable car
sell wares in the gorge
let us possess this city
we, who know what starving is
will feed the hungry.'

2.

postcard from Medillín
we, the poor, dictate the city.
packed solidly we put up our stalls.
if I sell a banana
it is something I have which is not nothing
at the green light
the motorcycles burst forth like cockroaches
big buses roar exhaust fumes
if you want to see tropical trees and clean air
dig in your pocket

postcard from Medillín
someone as old as my mother
as grey as my mother
pushes a pram
filled with cookies and tarts and sweets
plastic bags with cooldrink and fruit rolls.
what my mother gives in love
is bartered here for survival

postcard from Medillín
the dirtier the air
the cleaner the pavements
so many people you have never seen sweeping

postcard from Lampung
in the open sewer lies an enormous scapula
as if someone here ate a buffalo

postcard from Jakarta
in front of your Dutch mansion
I offer my bicycle taxi
and my friend: his motorcycle taxi
even a scooter if you want to go further.
at the two-wheel café we sell food to ourselves.
we laugh a lot when the others join us.
we throw the empty containers into the open sewer.
Hamsad has diarrhoea today.
when your 4X4 wants to get out we shift a little

postcard from Bandung
roasted hare
hang threaded
in the stalls
their hindlegs
long ribbons

postcard from Lampung
he pushes a two-wheel cart not bigger than a tray
on one side hangs a ruler-thin coal chest
on the other side five banana leaves and a flaming wick in a glass for light
he unties his chair – the size of a chequebook
he roasts five tiny satés over the thin line of coals
and serves them with rice-sausage in banana-leaf containers
in a space less than half a square meter
he feeds sixty people.

I need a room of my own
to write a poem

Every day I treat you as if you are mine

After two eighteenth-century engravings

When one crosses the equator everything becomes wilderness:
White becomes black, good becomes bad, culture becomes
A kind of barbarism in which nothing has a name:
Women throw a tit over the shoulder
Cannibals, winged lions, vulvas hanging down to the knees
Barking one-eyed people and snakes standing upright in trees.

Nobody will ever believe our relief when, one morning, we saw this
Table – something simply so miraculously ordinary in the wilderness
– something so civilised one at last could pin a memory there.
That's why, when we named it, we didn't want to honour any
God or king, but simply threw a moerse party
On the southern tip and baptised it 'Table Mountain'.

Because I had named you
I let you now rise somewhat higher in my engraving –
Up – like a real table. So that with you as backdrop we could throw
Our arms northward, we could stylise your skyline against the wilderness
And, as famous logo, bring you home
– we learnt quickly how the crumbs can fall from tables.

Neatly I draw your tabletop – nothing will hang skew.
To the side of the bay I put those who we say call themselves Hottentots.
They eat raw intestines and look! to have his cow give milk, this man
Blows into her bloody cunt. One has to know one's bearings, or what do
I say! To turn you into legend against the wilderness
I move you slightly more to the front – that's it, your feet closer to shore.

Windeberg and Leeukop, listen closely – throw your arms open
As if to embrace. To me it looks, and forgive me if I overestimate
Your reaching out, as if you and this continent groaneth and
Travaileth in pain until you could be delivered into glorious liberty
By the children of God. Every piece of property I will number and name
As it rises stepwise against your slopes –
Say what you want, but we did bring so much order to this place

That on my engraving I can have cultivated gardens
Blooming in the wilderness. And while I'm at it, let me show
The church in a larger scale. Next to the jetty, there, let's
Have the gallows – you never know, you know – this bay hangs
Full of heavily-laden ships anchoring at this place of Name.
For colour balance I smartly plant two flags flying over chaos.

Whatever this engraving adds and whatever it leaves out
However wide one casts the eye, however carefully one names,
Like Mandela you better be on our side, because out there, my dear,
the jungle claims!

Table Mountain and Table Bay were called Hoerikwaggo (Sea Mountain) and Camissa (Place of Sweet Waters) by the Khoi. Later arrivals alternatively named it Cabo da Boa Esperança (Cape of Good Hope), Golfo Dentro das Serras (Gulf within Mountains), Cape of Storms, Mons Mensa, Montagne de la Table, Tafelbergh, d'Klipman, Table Hill and Table Rock. In Zulu myth it was referred to as Umlindi Wemingizimu (Watcher of the South). Devil's Peak was also known as Windeberg and Herbert's Mount, while Leeuwenkop was once called Sugar Loafe.

During the past five hundred years, according to Nicolas Vergunst (*Hoerikwaggo – Images of Table Mountain*), Table Mountain has been likened to a fortress, a throne, an altar, a temple and God's anvil. It has been seen as a personification of a sleeping goddess, a giant and a towering Buddha, and described as a Fairyland, a Terrestrial Paradise and the Stairway to Heaven. It was the Portal to Africa, Watcher of the South, Guardian of the City, the Old Grey Father of colonialism and the Silent Witness of apartheid.

Mountain rondeau in four parts

1.

from inside   from outside
from in outside   from out inside
from innermost outside to outermost inside
from inner and outer namegivers to inner and outermost mountain

from inside Camissa from inside sweet water
from inside Camissa from outside fresh water
from innermost inside fresh water fresh sweet
from inside from outside

from outside Golfo   from outside Golfo Dentro
from outside Golfo Dentro das Serras from outside
from outside Golfo
from outside from inside

from inner outside from outer outside
from masterful namegivers of the mountain from the water
from outermost inside to innermost outside

I see a foyer   I see a guardian
I see a place   I see only sweet water
from inside from outside
from naming from taking
from refuge from subterfuge
from mountain from sea   from mountain as table
from inside from outside
from innermost inside from outermost inside

from hope   from apart
from apostle   from governor
from chief of taking   from chief of giving
from trade place from storm place
from god place from give place
from taking and taking
from taking

2.
from inside   from outside
from in outside   from out inside
from innermost outside to outermost inside
from inner and outer namegivers to inner and outermost mountain

from inside Camissa from inside sweet water
from inside Camissa from outside fresh water
from innermost inside fresh water fresh sweet
from inside from outside

from outside Golfo   from outside Golfo Dentro
from outside Golfo Dentro das Serras from outside
from outside Golfo
from outside from inside

from inside out from outside out
from masterful namegivers to the mountain from the water
from outermost inside to innermost outside

from Table Mountain Klipman   from outside Mons Mensa
from inside from outside
from inside out from outside in
from table of stone from inside from outside
Mons Mensa of stone and from outside
Mons Mensa of stone and from Mensa
Hoerikwaggo from inside from outside
from innermost outside Hoerikwaggo from outside
Hoerikwaggo from inside Hoerikwaggo from outside
Hoerikwaggo from innermost outside

without religion from outside
they are animals from inside
animals without souls from inside
from outside
without souls from inside
they're doomed from outside
have no rights from inside
acknowledged from outside

on land   on life
on living stock   on after life

3.
from inside   from outside
from in outside   from out inside
from innermost outside to outermost inside
from inner and outer namegivers to inner and outermost mountain

from inside Camissa from inside sweet water
from inside Camissa from outside fresh water
from innermost inside fresh water fresh sweet
from inside from outside

from outside Golfo   from outside Golfo Dentro
from outside Golfo Dentro das Serras from outside
from outside Golfo
from outside from inside

from inside out from outside out
from masterful namegivers to the mountain from the water
from outermost inside to innermost outside

Umlindi
Umlindi We
Umlindi Wemingizi
Umlindi Wemingizimu
from inside from outside
from innermost outside Umlindi
Umlindi Wemingizimu
Umlindi kwaggo
Hoeri Umlindi
Hoerikwaggo Umlindi
Umlindi Wemingizimu Hoerikwaggo Mons Mensa

mountains from outside are the world from inside
and outside is inside and inside now outside

some ascend mountains to see far
some ascend mountains to lay down the self
some ascend mountains to flee
some simply live on the slopes

some ascend mountains to test themselves
some ascend mountains to create borders
some ascend mountains to honour
some live in caves
simply on slopes

some ascend mountains to rule from there
some ascend mountains to chisel the gods
from in-less outside from out-less outside
outermost out-less outside
outermost out-less from outside

some live lightly on slopes
some only adore
some watch
how inside and outside are going to pieces

4.
from inside   from outside
from in outside   from out inside
from innermost outside to outermost inside
from inner and outer namegivers to inner and outermost mountain

from inside Camissa from inside sweet water
from inside Camissa from outside fresh water
from innermost inside fresh water fresh sweet
from inside from outside

from outside Golfo   from outside Golfo Dentro
from outside Golfo Dentro das Serras from outside
from outside Golfo
from outside from inside

inside out blows outside out
from outermost inside blows innermost outside
from outside blows inside
in-outside blow-inside
out-innermost out   blows outermost in
from blow-innerside outmost
from outblowerside inmost
from blust from blin
from blustblin minsside
blusside
blssd
blessed

PART THREE

Four seasonal observations of Table Mountain

AUTUMN

friday 8 may
fog falls like
a fainting spell. the mountain
fades to intimation
as wisps float free from black
umbrella pines. the mountain

has no form
no figure, no measure to
surrender. does it dress
in fathoms sunken silence or
petrify
stone by stone away from

a city
that disgusts it? chill rain slips
down its stony back. at noon
the gun fires. sound muffles
double
then fades into fog –

threads of fog.
fog plunges soundlessly from
the cliffs and drifts up
with the stench of kelp from

saturday 9 may
the bay. now
umbrella pines fall like
wet drawing pins from the
fog and are visible against the slopes
where the folds
still hold green before

dusk obliterates all
from the top down – until
only the wet street stays, a
window that steams
the colour of pumpkin soup.

my footsteps
crunch aloof, but the soundless
mountain has an absence
which the senses dare not impinge
upon. to
say the word mountain is

to compare
oneself to the mountain as
if we're endowed alike,
disfiguring the mountain in
its purest
self-sufficiency. in-
divisible
one; sad the time between

sunday 10 may
I try to ponder you: rock
hard, stone cold, everlastingly
aloof in
muted matting casings

until the
mass of umbrella pines fall
from scale, the foghorn moans
your absence into apprehension
that where you
are will ultimately

be one great
void.

monday 11 may

it moves . . . again –

(late afternoon)

confirmed –

mountain morning mounting

tuesday 12 may

the mountain throws off the clouds like
a cape and
stands radiant all at

once decked out
in wet stone like a
revelation in the
sun. then stacks its voice in the fullest
tones of stone
diapason and hymns

the purest sounds of
blinding blue. you're dazzled
with delight. triumphant
each echo

breaks to its
deepest hue – (forget the fog
rising up like a bad
conscience) o ye blesséd one who
listens to
unsurpasséd autumn

wednesday 13 may

blue. I lift
up mine eyes to the mountain
whence cometh my body?
my body comes from the mountain
which made arms
and heaven. the mountain

still remains
unaccountable. it throws
wide its arms and resounds
its cliffs with splendour over the
bay – holy
in immutable quartz

in the street
where I live I shall kneel with
my recidivist tongue:
o god of stone let me
not expire

thursday 14 may
early the city bowl
sloshes a brown
ring against the mountain
all along its stony throat
creep cloaks of decay. see
how it gasps
for something cool, lacking

something wild
of long ago when brushwood
nestled ferns at its feet
and clumps of trees cast cool shadows
when what came
to it across the bay

was a pure
explosion of oxygen,
light and loosely fragrant. o smell now
the odour
of the fouling fart of man.

friday 15 may
good morning
mountain, morning blue molar
chewing autumn rain's first
nimbular mash. hi furry plaque,
oh stony
gum, all infected with

cable-car
caries. hello stone enamel
worn-out by all-night light
as the city snores mouth agape
belching wind
past the exposed tooth necks.

good morning
you two old ground-down
incisors that stink more
and more in both directions. how
can one stay
unaffected while

legions squat on the tongue?
hello pustulant mould. hi
there tourist –
you're here too. see how you

saturday 16 may
milk us. yes, you.
for days the mountain guards its
autumn-bright throat; it glows
in all tones of stone – wrung through by
a pent-up

sunday 17 may
inner blue
that scorches through – as if the
core of the mountain is
vitreous blue, as if one stands
speechless that
blue in granite can

laze so loose,
in sandstone can swish so blue
across the bay, at dusk
can melt to such bluest deep
that from this
the water rocks

all day long
deeply intoxicated
and sifting in distant
lapidary sounds of soothsaying

monday 18 may
still you
slumber like
someone dozing on the beach –
your colours all your own:
the shale and the siltstone reddish
as it thrusts
through the scrub, in pewter
you lift up
your temples from sediment
and something glacial.
I have come to love you, yes, more
than I can

tuesday 19 may
bear. the leaves drift like dross.
the mountain
stands preserved in late quince light –
for your dark pink remoteness
I've come to care

WINTER

tuesday 17 june

after the storm
the mountain roars amber foam
down her fissures

wednesday 18 june

I cannot look at you
today, not today. with eyes averted
I do my daily chores. there
is no room left for the offer of
my voluntary self
to you in your stony perfection

over my terrified
body my hand moves again up to
my breast again hoping
that the lump of clay will not be there
that the hand misconstrued
that it has indeed vanished in the

meantime. the mountain stands
stripped clean and burnt through. I live by the
breath of the mountain alone.
I have no other competence. on
the windward side fringes of light sing, on
the lee side there is nought

not even a single
line that knows of me. mortality
sticks to my lip like sweat.
I want to know/not to know/to know
everything/know nothing

thursday 19 june

invisible mountain
in the mist – a lump of grief against
which everything flounders.
softly your thoughts try to probe around
it gently you sense the
embedded stone, the numbness of it

the immobility,
you don't have the courage to fathom
the full extent, you just
await the result. from the waist you
blindly suppose yourself
secretly whole, you try to defuse

your body's insurgence
against your body. let the stone lump
grow cold in the fog, let
the pine trees tilt like umbrellas in
a cortège, let my thoughts
steam to ripeness in sorrow. but I,

I am occupied this
morning: softly I coax my breasts to
unwind in foam, let them
freely drowse in tranquil fragrance, then
I rinse them in honey
to luminous shape and there where the

mammogram reveals its
blackest clot, I lather in light, I
caress with the sweetest
tonality of breath, of light-limbed
tintinnabulous bliss
there the light soaks in so blindingly

that the black membrane feels
itself blessed by blue, diluting its
viscous toxic polyps,
dissolving them to effluence. see
the rust bleed like biestings
from my nipples. Whole like a whiplash

I *want* to live on this earth.

(late night)

fuck-all. I feel fuck-all
for the life hereafter – it's *now* that
I want to live, *here* that

I want to live. when I
look at you I grow sad, oh yes as
sad as the heart can see

it's because I'm mortal that you're
so goddam lovely. I want to be

eternally mortal.

sunday 22 june

nothing arrives. my throat
constricts. a resigned grief burns up in
my chest, smoking. my heart
whimpers on her hinges. I want to
touch something, hold something,
revive the wholeness that once was mine.

I want to return with
my previous body. I am not
I, without my body
only through my body can I in-
habit this earth. my soul
is my body entire. my body

embodies what I am.
do not turn against me, oh do not
ever leave me. do not
cave in around me, do not plummet
away from me, do not
die off on me, do not leave me with-
out testimony. I
have a body, therefore I am. step
into the breach for me –
yes, you are my only mandate to
engage the earth in love.

monday 23 june

scot-free   I no longer have to
dwell on the word 'malignant', it's
the word 'benign'
that makes my skin slip like a gorgeous
silk scarf round my body.
I breathe freely. the air has quickened.

I drink my morning tea. my
eyes consume the mountain in stately
gait, but something, what I
do not know, has surfaced quietly –
in deadly silence it
encrusts the windows – everything feels

circumscribed to preserve
it from extinction. to prevent you
from falling into your hair, you trace the mountain.
mortal, the entire world
hangs suddenly or shrieks in fragments.

on the counterpane your
perimeters eventually fade,
your presence will be wiped
one morning like dust from a bookshelf.
without a body you
will not survive anywhere. even

after death your body can still
be held in photographs
your pulse beats free
like a prisoner just escaped, but
mortality's come on
board. the body starts taking its leave.

friday 27 june

the last rains of winter fall
faster than yearning or winter trees
with lymphatic systems
against the wintry light. it's as if
I am young again in
my upper arms suddenly, and smooth

at the back of my head.
my body glows complete, my elbows
hang free with my senses
extended over my skin. I see
the mountain, maintaining
herself on her cliffs, containing her-

self in stone as stone, her-
self complete in herself. she decays
with the earth in the tongue
of eternity. I can do nought
but ascend in her with
roaring immaculate radiance

SPRING

wednesday 8 september

nothing as
green as the unblemished large
first green flakes of oak trees
in the spring and the mountain a
sheaf of blue
fragrance. oh say it now!

thursday 9 september

this morning she withdraws
herself from speech. she refuses to
broach herself. her breasts of
stone she still conceals with copious
steaming wings like when it
rained on and on for a thousand years

the mountain declines to
be dislodged from her cliff – toothless she
grumbles in the fog, yet
when she does lift her kaross for an
instant, sinew-white a
newborn waterfall flashes to light

friday 10 september

I try to remain
standing upright and singing. the clouds
gather round the longer
living and weld along her seams: quick-
silver soldering joints

she strides into springtime –
her lintels are rinsed, her gutters are
green, her thresholds flowering forth:

– see how the heart polishes her stoep
– how joy suffuses the mammary glands

saturday 11 september
early on
the mountain releases all
the shades that it gathered
by night – through the day it stockpiles
them with thrift
in ridges of blue-bayed range

sunday 12 september
it plays in
light and shade. it mulls in clouds
of spring. the mountain
suddenly senses itself laced
in strings
of birdsong. before the

day is in
full flight, the mountain hoists it-
self above the salute
of white gables, bougainvillea
that droop shelves
of burning embers on

the railings.
and from the hibiscuses
pistils clapper amongst
threads of pollen. overblown blue-
gum trees drone
on with bee buzz and ash.

the mountain
feels sprightly this morning as
it shudders the damp chill
from its dewlap and its broad grinning
smile reaches
deep to its wrong-headed skull

monday 20 september

oh
oh the
oh the awesome comfort
oh the absolutely awesome comfort
            of my breasts

wednesday 22 september

your tabletop
reveals the stratified sediment
layers of your ancient
origin. of all the mountains
you have changed
the least. from the very

top of your
enormous blocks of sand-
stone you step down in steps
to the blushing siltstone of Graaf-
water. all
rest compact on granite

and on smooth
distilled magma. what do you
recall, reliquary
of time? does the molten earth core
still hide as
squirting sound somewhere in

your stone? or
does an igneous layer
protect the whirring of
ferns and sightless invertebrates?
does something still
quiver after the sand

deposits
petrified down to seven
hundred meters? or is
it the severing from the other
continent
forty million years back

that makes you
endure unyieldingly over
the bay? that was the day,
they say, that all the stone in you
cracked. that part, as you know,
never returns to one.

saturday 25 september
this morning the mountain
is all commotion: she shakes out her
fynbos carpets in the
sun where the flowers, clicking like jewels,
gulp air. the silver trees in
dressing gowns she urges up

Lion's Head, she scrubs her
ravines green, threads fine strings of water
into each gorge. even
stone gets its cover of sunlight
in spring. her ledges she
dusts and thrusts her breasts in
the pristine sun. she has
no truck with the hordes of eyes ogling
her body. she is
filled with reservoirs, shade for breathing
and hollows for dewfall.
dawdling, she beckons to life

friday 1 october
does maiden-
hair plunge down to earth?

and does wild
flax flower under

the lack of
speech? do restios

still reek of
kidneys, is sorrel

labile when
colour curls from its

lap? does royal
heath thrive only else-

where? do we
inhabit the land

unlidded
among blood flowers?

saturday 2 october
1.
you walk in through my windows
and you talk into my eyes
I take you daily like an oath but
inevitably you too are heading for

rack and ruin – but you don't weather
like man but with the language of the
earth – cautiously I pay tribute with
the fingertips of umbrella pines

2.
in your privileged embrace I dwell

but thousands on your outskirts survive
on a different silhouette

for how many aeons will you yet
observe how we settle the case?

sunday 3 october
steadily the days curve
more brightly over me. the blossoms
are crushed by the wind. on
some inclines I shall never saunter
again. from the earliest
times you have been identified daily

and appropriated with
eyes and inhalations. only in
some imaginations
are you methodically flaked off.
my heart knows that you have
nothing to do with us, that you are

lost deep in the concept
of mountain, that the word mountain is
an abstract noun, that blue
is a verb, stone a friend, for next to
you I become she and
she he and we irrevocably

become us, because you
remain you. all in-
cantations of yearning
tilt in my chest. my pulse resounds with
poems and axillary
feathers, my blazing gizzard

buzzes with rhyme. I hone
my heart to yours. I shall never let
you leave me. words my mouth
will lose – my seams will be undone – I
speak many tongues but not
one of them any longer my own

SUMMER

thursday 18 november

the mountain
this morning looks like never
before as if it hides
already behind white muslin
cloth, as if
it stands veiled, as if it
is painted décor

friday 17 december

oh tell me
my mother, does brown gonna
draw moths like a flame at
dusk? does featherhead smell fair? how
still is pink
stilbe? is bels herb brewed to

brandy and
blombos to honey? can one
draw wood-bleach from sorrel
in the wee hours when the mountain
whispers like
a dark woollen wimple?

saturday 18 december

like a big
flickering butterfly of stone
the mountain quivers

in the heat.
the city bowl shrieks like a hot
cauldron. your breath breaks

into flames.
searing, the cicadas singe the
peripheries black.

behind a
gas flame the mountain rages with
heat, with fire, with a

scorching blaze
of hatred. are you perhaps in
a basket of shade,

or in the
purple silver breath of a wild
olive tree? is the

light sweat on
your upper lip a sacrifice
to allow you to

kneel down with
both your knees planted on the earth?
let its will be done

sunday 22 january
fog already steals across the bay.
Blouberg's point bleeds into the
sky. it looks as if a white powder puff
is shaken out, as
if rhinoceros grass evinces a

haze, as if the mountain
groans in the heat. the helicopter
whips up a thimble of
water from the reservoir, and fades
into smoke round Devil's
Peak – just to swerve jauntily over

the bay and cool its sting
in the sea. the city bowl drones. the
air smells of pyres.
with sheer sounds the starlings swoop
from the loquat tree
rooted in front of my window.

monday 23 january
when the mountain again
licked his magnificent face clean this
morning, I'd had enough
of fucking eternity. come try
and feel *human* time for
a change: to piss him off on purpose

I spilt little slops of
cloud over the edge to make them slide
down helter-skelter and
vanish right in front of his eyes. and
then I picked up speed. I
pumped him full of clouds that gasped round his
nipples with sensuous abandon

and just when the poor old
sod thought I wanted to snog, I jumped
him and cooked his goose till
white foam splashed shamelessly from his top
I rushed at his jowls and
ripped his moustache out of the way like

a mat; like a gangster
I gave him lip and cut his thighs to
mush. casually I slapped
his cheek because I *wanted* him to
panic, but all he did
was stare at Robben Island

then I pummelled
more viciously and when he opened
that gob to bitch, I slapped
with my flat hand to make his snot burst
(fuck what a superb sound
of pulp). then I wanted to *hear*: I

grabbed his balls till he
squealed. come! you bloody coward, come *live*
for just a few decades! at
first he drew back but then I whacked his
head till his eardrums burst.
I ripped his skin from his

armpits, hacked connections
of red and white glands from his neck and
twisted my blade deep in
his right kidney: I want to see him
mortal, crapping with fear

tuesday 24 january
violence pours from me. my feet keep

pounding till it fades and
my brain turns blind. I throw my weight dead
like a ploughshare into his
back, I want god knows to wipe him out
till he lifts my sentence
and acquits me from death. I'm frenzied

with anger because I
live only once, because in all of
eternity I live
only *now*, because I only *start*
to live now, because I
shall live through this earthly glory just
once with this body, and
my body is fading already
in spasms of
            evermore, nevermore, neverlasting

wednesday 25 january
yet the
mountain still stares across the sea.
it rides me out like a
storm, breaks me to a breeze, and makes
me flow at
water level to its

girth; when I
calm down, it skims the pointed
pivot of silence over
the bay – a dove gives it breath, and
a falcon
spreads the far-flung wingspan

thursday 26 january

between the mountain and the wild muttering roses
the perforated eardrum of the poem festers,
growing word by word more deaf. write
that the summer has stilled, spell the day without wind,
read from haziness like a lover
that extracts heat from the air. it's a sweltering
day. translate the writing in a bell chiming
from shadow to shadow through the neck of a stanza
and write how the body exists, how it surfaces
as slendered stone ever looking inward
to the silence. write how our eyes dwell on it to read
what is written there, how the summer air stains verse
on the mountain because blue is the most wind-blown
letter and the most illegible sound.

saturday 28 january

you unleash
the southeaster with so much
loathing on us while you
reign fragile as glass – oh the wind
rages
and rattles the roof

raps against
the windows like one who wants
to enter, who wants to
destroy, who wants to sweep us in-
to the sea –
and then one morning how

still is it
when the wind dies down – who can
express it stiller than
the turtle-dove? who more movingly
than the leaf-still
wind-blown trees above?

sunday 29 january

from the summit
the mountain closes in, the
streams grow wetter and the
leaves more sodden, disa secrets
burst into
rush and dew. at first I

thought of you
as male, as blue-blood cliché
but see how this morning
my arms grasp to hold a woman
sternly emboused in blue

monday 30 january

the sun pours
heat down your upper
arms – you feel loved and long-
limbed. unimpeded the mountain
gazes down
to the oven in her

lap. you are
utterly unaware that
the first chill of autumn
has as bondsman submitted the
end of you through the soles of your feet

the mountain
stays the other   absolute

tuesday 31 january

I stretch out my palms to
pull the image of the mountain in-
to my arms, the mountain
into whose spell I look up daily.
benevolent the sun,
steady the colour of stone with rust
stains here and there as if
scales had to be scraped off. the higher
the stonier it gets
with old bald patches and a sudden
green fingerprint top right.
if I look across the bay against

the sun with you, every
sugarbush gleams a flame pink light bulb.
your stone remembers when
the earth was still soft to the touch and
you were silver rinsed clean
and left ripped away. your

stone remembers when the
first creeping beast ascended you; your
fynbos remembers when
you were alone, just you and the wind
and the blue white bay; your
shape remembers the exact moment
when a human eye first
beheld you and you had to become
involved involved in time

thursday 2 february

unyielding she keeps her
stone amassed. between distribution
and redistribution,
advantage and previously disad-
vantaged she keeps her cool,
because the more she's abused for loot

or ideology,
the more she moults and shakes herself clean;
the more the arrogant
die against her cliffs, roads and suburbs and
detours choke up against
her, the stronger the wind she rams down

her kloofs – the decay of
human memory evidently
insignificant on
her face.

friday 3 february

just when they think she is theirs,
she heaves her mighty head
scornfully erect to the sky and

reveals her body in a
resounding triumph of
mountain. majestic she stands there, clamorous
in a fucking larynx of radiant

ruin – my god, I am
covered in goosebumps. this she will do long
after I'd fallen back from her
finally

– de-heavened

Translated by Andries Wessels

Acknowledgments

The acknowledgment of sources in poetry has undergone radical change in recent years. Previously it was the task of academics and reviewers to discover the sources and apply them as context. Now the onus is completely on the poet to stipulate that she doesn't want her readers to think that every poem has had a 'virgin birth'.

Let me say then that these poems are filled with echoes, lines and words from other Afrikaans poets. I cannot write without them. In recent years the work of Hugo Claus, Gerrit Kouwenaar and many other Dutch poets have also influenced my poetry. So have the poems of Adrienne Rich, Dylan Thomas and Paul Celan. In this volume I have, in addition, used lines from *The Selected Poetry of Yehuda Amichai* (translated by Chana Bloch and Stephen Mitchell, University of California Press, 1996) – 'marital song 1'; and from *Blood, Tin, Straw* by Sharon Olds (Cape Poetry, Jonathan Cape, 2000) – 'marital song 2'; 'morning tea' is a gendered response to Rutger Kopland's *Onder de Appelboom*; the poem also incorporates three words by Rita Dove that I heard during a poetry reading but have not yet seen in printed form; echoes of W.B. Yeats's 'A Prayer for Old Age' can be found in 'Dommelfei'. For the titles 'leave me a lonely began' and 'softsift' I am indebted to Gerard Manley Hopkins, and for the visual presentation of Part Three to the way Bleek and Lloyd recorded '//Kabbo's Death on the hunting ground' (Bleek and Lloyd Collection, Jagger Library, University of Cape Town).

Other books that influenced this volume are: *Conversations with Difference* by the Indonesian philosopher and poet Goenawan Mohamad (Pt Tempo Inti Media, Tbk, Jakarta, 2002), *Women's Bodies, Women's Wisdom* by Dr Christiane Northrup, (Piatkus, London, 1998) and *Hoerikwaggo – Images of Table Mountain* by Nicolaas Vergunst. My admiration for Dommelfei comes from *Mario en die Diere* by Waldemar Bonsels (translated from the German by A.E. Carinus, J.L. van Schaik, Pretoria, 1939). And of course The Bible.

Many thanks to Chateau de L'Avigny where I wrote most of the 'body' poems, and to Bellagio where the Table Mountain poems were given shape. Thank you also to Helvitia and the special travel fund of Bellagio who covered my travel costs. My deepest thanks however goes to Hazel Moolman, David Goldblatt and Gus Ferguson for his impeccable, sensitive and intelligent reading, as well as his tireless efforts to focus a text.

The English text sometimes differs from the original Afrikaans in content and/or form. This is the case where the translation process required creative solutions, which in their turn opened up other possibilities in the poems. All translations were done by me, except for 'manifesta of a grandma' and 'Four seasonal observations of Table Mountain', done by Andries Wessels, and 'it might have been a jellytot', done by Gus Ferguson. The final draft of all the translations was however thoroughly scrutinised by Gus, Andries, me and my publisher Annari van der Merwe. Andries Wessels is professor of English at the University of Pretoria and Gus Ferguson a poet and pharmacist.